Mini Lop Rabbits as Pets

The Handy Guide for Mini Lop Rabbits

Mini Lop Rabbit General Info, Purchasing, Care, Marketing, Keeping, Health, Supplies, Food, Breeding and More Included!

By: Lolly Brown

Copyrights and Trademarks

All rights reserved. No part of this book may be reproduced or transformed in any form or by any means, graphic, electronic, or mechanical, including photocopying, recording, taping, or by any information storage retrieval system, without the written permission of the author.

This publication is Copyright ©2019 NRB Publishing, an imprint. Nevada. All products, graphics, publications, software and services mentioned and recommended in this publication are protected by trademarks. In such instance, all trademarks & copyright belong to the respective owners. For information consult www.NRBpublishing.com

Disclaimer and Legal Notice

This product is not legal, medical, or accounting advice and should not be interpreted in that manner. You need to do your own due-diligence to determine if the content of this product is right for you. While every attempt has been made to verify the information shared in this publication, neither the author, neither publisher, nor the affiliates assume any responsibility for errors, omissions or contrary interpretation of the subject matter herein. Any perceived slights to any specific person(s) or organization(s) are purely unintentional.

We have no control over the nature, content and availability of the web sites listed in this book. The inclusion of any web site links does not necessarily imply a recommendation or endorse the views expressed within them. We take no responsibility for, and will not be liable for, the websites being temporarily unavailable or being removed from the internet.

The accuracy and completeness of information provided herein and opinions stated herein are not guaranteed or warranted to produce any particular results, and the advice and strategies, contained herein may not be suitable for every individual. Neither the author nor the publisher shall be liable for any loss incurred as a consequence of the use and application, directly or indirectly, of any information presented in this work. This publication is designed to provide information in regard to the subject matter covered.

Neither the author nor the publisher assume any responsibility for any errors or omissions, nor do they represent or warrant that the ideas, information, actions, plans, suggestions contained in this book is in all cases accurate. It is the reader's responsibility to find advice before putting anything written in this book into practice. The information in this book is not intended to serve as legal, medical, or accounting advice.

Foreword

Owning and keeping rabbits is not just a fun thing to do, it's also very rewarding in the long run. However, in terms of costs and overall caring, it requires long – term commitment and can be quite a huge responsibility. If you are thinking about a rabbit or two even on a temporary basis, it's required by law to ensure that their basic needs are met as well as implementation of proper husbandry practices.

There's no such thing as a perfect or linear way of caring for rabbits because they vary in breed, sizes, and also personality. As a potential keeper, it's up to you on how you're going to look after your pet bunnies and ensure that you take reasonable steps in doing so.

The biology and also the behavior of the mini lop rabbits is quite similar to its relatives under the lop family but in general domestic rabbits have the same characteristics as wild rabbits which means that they can have complex needs. Rabbits particularly mini lops are great pets for young kids and the young – at – hearts, learn how you can properly care for them by reading this book and treating it as sort of a pet owner's manual that will guide you in your journey as a responsible bunny keeper.

Table of Contents

Introduction 1

Chapter One: The Mini Lops' Origin Story 2

    Taxonomy and Description 3

    Physical Characteristics.. 3

    Breed Status 4

    Mini Lop Rabbit Colors 5

    Lifespan 7

        Causes of Short Lifespan.. 7

    History of Miniature Lops 8

        Quick Facts.. 10

Chapter Two: Costs and Commitment of Keeping Mini Lops
.... 12

    Requirements and Costs of Keeping a Rabbit 13

        Initial Set Up Costs for Rabbits 15

        Maintenance Costs:... 17

    Mini Lop Rabbit Personality.. 21

Chapter Three: Handling, Housing, and Feeding.................. 24

    A Hutch and a Home for Your Mini Lops 26

        A Sanitary Shelter 29

    Companionship for Your Mini Lops................................... 29

    Holidays and Transportations 30

- Rabbit Companions 31
  - How to Introduce Rabbits to Each Other 32
- Nutrition Guidelines for Your Pet 35
  - Nutritious Food and Fresh Water 36
  - Commercial Pellet Diet 37
  - Work with Your Vet for Diet 39
- Feeding Tips and Measurements 40
  - Adult – Sized Mini Lop Diet 40
  - Treats 41
  - Young Mini Lop Rabbits for Diet 42
- How to Pick – Up Rabbits 43

Chapter Four: Behavior and Bunny Quirks 46

- Mini Lop Bunny Behavior 47
  - Hiding Places 48
  - Play Time 49
  - Digging and Chin Marking 50
  - Keep them Safe! 51
- Bunny Quirks 52

Chapter Five: Breeding Basics and Culling 56

- Breeding for Rabbitries 57
- Sorting Litters 62
  - Basics of Culling Mini Lop Rabbits 63

Chapter Six: Showing Your Mini Lop Rabbits 68

   Breed Standard 69

      Standard of Perfection 70

      Coat Colors and Patterns 72

      Coat Type 84

Chapter Seven: Health and Welfare 85

   Health Check 86

      Life Expectancy 86

   Spay and Neuter Surgeries 87

   Medical Emergencies 88

   Grooming and Other Health Concerns 88

   GI Stasis: A Very Common Illness of Rabbits 92

   Glossary of Rabbit Terms 98

Index 102

Photo Credits 110

References 112

Introduction

Rabbits in general are active and fun creatures; they have this innate quality to run, jump, dig or hop. They must have the freedom to roam or skip around, and have a place to rest. As a potential rabbit keeper, it's your job to give them a conducive environment to live in where they can have frequent opportunities to play and exercise, happily live their lives without fear of any potential threats, and have enough space to keep them healthy, happy, and safe.

Rabbits also tend to easily get scared which is why you may need to provide a "safe place" for them within their hutch or enclosure because even if they're literally safe, they still might get stress because they don't have a private place to go to. The potential threats to these fluffy creatures are

Introduction

bigger household pets like dogs, cats, parrots, reptiles and other bigger animals in general. If ever you happen to also be a keeper of other household pets then make sure to not let them get anywhere near to your rabbits' place because it might cause stress and fear to your pet rabbits.

Mini Lop rabbits in particular are smart creatures and require mental and physical stimulation which is why it's best to provide them with toys and 'obstacles' they can play with. The downside to rabbit keeping aside from cleaning their litter is that they may suffer from boredom so make sure that they're always occupied. It's also your duty to make your home (and your rabbit's hutch) hazard – free because their curiosity might get the best of them. Rabbits usually injure themselves so it's better to bunny – proof their environment.

In addition to providing them with their basic requirements, what you will learn from this book is their biological and behavioral characteristics because all of these will come in handy especially when your rabbit gets sick or is acting differently.

If you're planning to eventually become a breeder or acquire more than one Mini Lop, then you need to make sure that you can have enough attention, and money to care for the litters' needs. Breeding and showing rabbits are also something that we're going to touch on later in this book.

Introduction

This book will contain useful information on how to properly care for your pet Mini Lop rabbit. We will provide you with practical tips on how to keep your pet active, healthy, and also happy! Get ready to turn into mush because the Mini Lop breed will surely give you cuteness overload!

Introduction

Chapter One: The Mini Lops' Origin Story

Under the Animal Welfare Act, pet keepers in general are obliged to make sure that they care for their pet's basic welfare needs. Such needs include a suitable environment to live, a healthy diet, clean and fresh water to drink, and also protection from any pain or suffering from potential threats including people, other animals, diseases and household hazards. This chapter will focus on the mini lops' origin story and physical characteristics. You'll get to know where they came from, what their physical attributes are, their domesticated purpose, their current breed status as well as their lifespan and available colors.

Chapter One: The Mini Lops' Origin Story

Taxonomy and Description

The scientific name of Miniature Lop rabbits or Mini Lops is *Oryctolagus cuniculus*. It originated in Germany and is the same breed as a Holland Lop rabbit. It was recognized by the American Rabbit Breeders Association (ARBA) in 1980 and this breed is also available in various coats or colors.

Mini Lop rabbits have two nicknames in the U.S.; they are called "Monarch of the Fancy," and "Lops of Excellence." In the U.K., the British Rabbit Council (BRC) is known as the "Dwarf Lop." They are technically Holland Lop breeds but the difference is that the mini lops are quite smaller in size but has a heavier weight than the Holland lops, though they have much longer ears than their parent breed. In the U.S. there are 2 official Mini Lop breed clubs; these are the Mini Lop Rabbit Club of America, and the American Mini Lop Rabbit Club.

Physical Characteristics

Miniature Lop rabbits are one of the smallest breeds of bunnies in the world. Its maximum weight is only around 6 ½ pounds but despite of its small size, their body structure is stocky. These rabbits have a compact and sturdy body

Chapter One: The Mini Lops' Origin Story

with short neck. Lop breeds in general doesn't have erect ears compared to other rabbit breeds; with the mini lops, their furry rounded tipped ears are resting on the sides of their head just like their other lop relatives. The fur of miniature lops have a normal length and its under layer coat is plush that's covered with longer guard fur. Their coat is also rolled back which means that it can normally return to position whenever it is brushed backward.

Newbie keepers often get confused between a Miniature Lop and a Holland Lop; as mentioned earlier the best indicator is their weight but other than that mini lops are still Holland lop breeds, they are just referred to as mini lops due to their size/ weight. The related breeds include the French Lop, Polish Lop, Chinchilla, New Zealand Lop, and Dwarf Lop.

Mini lops are bred as a show breed and also a domesticated household pet.

Breed Status

Mini lops are quickly becoming a popular rabbit breed particularly in the U.S. and in the U.K. Many keepers are also becoming more and more interested in breeding Mini Lops.

Chapter One: The Mini Lops' Origin Story

Mini Lop Rabbit Colors

The American Rabbit Breeders Association recognizes various types of coat colors for Mini Lop rabbits. Later in the Showing Chapter, we'll discuss more about the coat colors and patterns that's qualified for show. These colors are categorized into seven groups/ patterns, they are as follows:

Agouti

- Chinchilla (Blue, Lilac, Black, Smoke Pearl, Chocolate and Sable)
- Lynx
- Opal
- Chestnut Agouti

Pointed White

- Black
- Chocolate
- Lilac
- Blue

Broken

- Broken
- Tri – Colored

Chapter One: The Mini Lops' Origin Story

Self

- Lilac
- Blue
- White
- Chocolate
- Black

Shaded

- Seal
- Sable
- Frosted Pearl
- Smoke Pearl
- Tortoise
- Sable Point

Ticked

- Silver
- Steel
- Silver Fox

Wide Band

- Cream
- Orange/ Fawn
- Red

Chapter One: The Mini Lops' Origin Story

Lifespan

The average life span of mini lops is around 8 to 10 years. Some of these breeds have been known to live well beyond their average lifespan provided that you practice proper husbandry and you provide your pet with tender love and care. Usually, mini lops and other small rabbit breeds are prone to an illness called maloclussion as well as other common diseases so if you want your rabbit to live a long and healthy life make sure that their health is being taken care of.

Causes of Short Lifespan

Rabbits in general don't live longer if they are housed indoors compared to those that are free to roam outside, although indoor bunnies are less likely to be injured or catch any common diseases, their true habitat is found in nature.

Sometimes rabbits that do not have companions are most likely to die early because they either get bored by themselves or because they feel alone especially if they live indoors.

Indoor rabbits also tend to suffer due to improper nutrition; this is usually not the owner's fault especially if rabbits are being given with the right amount of diet, it's

Chapter One: The Mini Lops' Origin Story

more of a behavioral thing and this is known as GI stasis. This happens when indoor rabbits aren't given the freedom to forage their own food and are given with diets that's either too high in calories or quite low in fiber.

This is the reason why it's probably best that you house your mini lop rabbit/s outside because outside in nature is where they truly belong but if that's not possible due to the fact that they could escape or they could face potential threats then it's best to just keep them indoors but perhaps just give them time to freely roam around the house or your backyard with supervision.

History of Miniature Lops

In 1972, there was a rabbit show in Essen, Germany known as the German National Rabbit show, and this is where Bob Herschbach first sighted the cute Mini Lop breed. The first mini lops are locally known in Germany as Klein Widder, and this breed is the offspring of a Chinchilla breed and a German Big Lop rabbits; these 2 breeds are originally white and Agouti in color.

The German Big Lop has a weight of around 8 pounds. It also has large and thick ears that mini lops still possess today. Herschbach became fascinated with the result of combining the small Chinchilla breed and the German Big

Chapter One: The Mini Lops' Origin Story

Lop, and because of this he wanted to promote the newfound breed in America. He eventually procreated the Miniature Lop rabbits in the U.S. around 1972, and he was the first one to do so. He did it by pairing up a white female lop with the offspring of an Agouti – colored lop rabbits. The first ever litter of baby mini lops were solid in colors but on the second generation, it came with broken colors. As years go by, rabbit breeders eventually became successful in obtaining a high – standard physical characteristic that we see today in the modern Mini Lops.

Two years later after seeing this breed, the Mini Lop rabbits of Herschbach were shown in the ARBA convention that was held in California. However, the organization suggested that for this breed to be officially recognized, it needs to be downsized to a more compact size and the breed name should be replaced from Klein Widder to "Mini Lop" so that it'll be more appealing to the public. What Herschbach did to achieve the size that the organization want is to ask the help of other American breeders. He let the other breeders breed more of his original mini lops to achieve the desired compact size.

In 1977, the breed was under a new sponsorship and Herb Dyke is the one in charge to promote this new breed. In 1978, both Dyke and Herschbach created a rabbit club for the Mini Lop breed, and within just a year, the Mini Lop attracted lots of rabbit enthusiasts from various states. Over a thousand members supported the new breed. Finally in

Chapter One: The Mini Lops' Origin Story

1980, the Mini Lop rabbit was officially recognized as an official rabbit breed by the American Rabbit Breeders Association at the National Rabbit Convention held in Milwaukee, Wisconsin. In the same year, the Mini Lop Club of America was also established.

Quick Facts

Origin: Germany

Pedigree: offspring of a German Big Lop and Chinchilla; also related to Holland Lop

Breed Size: small - sized breed

Body Type and Appearance: Has a compact and sturdy body type. Has proportionate legs, round eyes, hanged - down ears that are large and has rounded tips, has relatively small head and comes in various color.

Group/s: American Rabbit Breeders Association (ARBA), The British Rabbit Council (BRC), the Mini Lop Club of America

Weight: The weight must not exceed 6 ½ pounds.

Coat Length: short coated breed

Coat Texture: short and soft

Chapter One: The Mini Lops' Origin Story

Color: Blue, Lilac, Black, Smoke Pearl, Chocolate, Sable among others.

Temperament: quite laid back, friendly, sociable, trainable, not that active but still needs mental stimulation

Strangers: friendly around strangers

Other Rabbits: generally good with other rabbit breeds if properly introduced, trained, and socialized.

Other Pets: generally friendly with other pets but shouldn't be left with other huge animals because it might get scared since rabbits are mostly prey animals.

Exercise Needs: provide toys for mental and physical stimulation and a space they can roam around in.

Lifespan: approximately 8 to 10 years

Chapter Two: Costs and Commitment of Keeping Mini Lops

This chapter will tackle the estimated costs that's involved in keeping mini lops, and rabbits in general. It will give you an idea of the kind of commitment that current rabbit owners and potential keepers like yourself will have to experience in terms of both the time and attention required as well as the overall financial expenses. The estimated costs and figures that you'll learn in this chapter were derived from various rabbit experts including breeders, vets, and animal welfare.

Chapter Two: Costs and Commitment of Keeping Mini Lops
Requirements and Costs of Keeping a Rabbit

It's important to note that the estimated figures provided in this chapter refer to the time and financial costs for single mini lops and also for pairs of healthy mini lops. If ever your pet happens to have a health or behavior problem then expect that the vet consultations, training, and medical procedures involve are likely to cost much more than the average.

Estimated Time (and Attention) Required for a Pair of Healthy Mini Lops

The time and attention required for both indoor and outdoor rabbits are thought to be quite the same.

Daily rabbit routine includes the following:
- Feeding and providing clean, fresh water
- Cleaning toilet or litter area
- Basic health check
- Time for exercise opportunities or playful activity that requires the supervision of the keeper (this includes supervision in the backyard, garden or rabbit – proofed spaces).
- Daily interaction with the mini lop/s.

Chapter Two: Costs and Commitment of Keeping Mini Lops

Important Note:
- Experts recommend that the exercise/ play area of the rabbits should be permanently attached to the main hutch or enclosure so that the mini lops can have the freedom to be out any time they want.

- If the mini lop needs to be kept without other rabbit companies for welfare reasons then you as the owner should make sure that you spend more time interacting with your pet mini lop every single day to provide companionship otherwise your pet could become lonely and eventually get stressed out.

The estimated minimum time that owners need to allot per day both for single and paired rabbits is 1 full hour. Do take note, however that the time required to complete the tasks aforementioned might take more than an hour especially if you need to groom or clean the cage of your pet rabbit.

Weekly rabbit activities may include the following:
- Cleaning the hutch or enclosure
- Grooming (since mini – lops are short haired, grooming can be done at least once a week)
- Body and behavior check (to see if the rabbit is well – rounded and generally healthy)
- Interaction

Chapter Two: Costs and Commitment of Keeping Mini Lops

The time and attention required for both indoor and outdoor rabbits per week are 10 hours. However, it could take much longer if your mini lop/s is either sick or have other issues.

Initial Set Up Costs for Rabbits

Costs	Expense for 1 (Outdoor Rabbit)	Expense for 2 (Outdoor Rabbits)	Expense for 1 (Indoor Rabbit)	Expense for 2 (Indoor Rabbit)
Adoption Fee or Purchase Price (If you plan on adopting, the fee may already cover medical costs like vaccinations, neutering, and micro – chipping, and overall vet health check)	$32 (£25)	$65 (£50)	$32 (£25)	$65 (£50)
Neutering	$103 (£80)	$207 (£160)	$103 (£80)	$207 (£160)
Microchipping	$32 (£25)	$65 (£50)	$32 (£25)	$65 (£50)

Chapter Two: Costs and Commitment of Keeping Mini Lops

1st Vaccinations (usually require 2 visits) and vet routine check up	$65 (£50)	$129 (£100)	$65 (£50)	$129 (£100)
Accommodation (includes main shelter and play pen)	$453 (£350) This includes: Hutch/ Playpen/ Shed/ Fence/ Other rabbit – proof materials		$323 (£250) This includes: Indoor hutch/ Playpen/ Other rabbit – proof materials	
Equipment: • Water Bowl and Water Bottle	$10 (£8)	$10 (£8)	$10 (£8)	$10 (£8)
• Food Dispenser (hayrack and food balls)	$10 (£8)	$15 (£12)	$10 (£8)	$15 (£12)
• Hiding Places, Platforms, Litter Trays, Toys	$15 (£12)	$25 (£20)	$15 (£12)	$25 (£20)

Mini Lops as Pets

Chapter Two: Costs and Commitment of Keeping Mini Lops

• Grooming Materials	$15 (£12)	$15 (£12)	$15 (£12)	$15 (£12)
• Travel Carrier (good for 2 rabbits)	$52 (£40)	$52 (£40)	$52 (£40)	$52 (£40)
Total:	$780 (£610)	$1,038 (£802)	$660 (£510)	$907 (£701)

Maintenance Costs:

Costs	Expense for 1 Rabbit (Indoor/Outdoor)	Expense for 1 Rabbit (Indoor/Outdoor)
Food • Hay (includes bedding)	$19 (£15) per week $77 (£60) per month $932 (£720) per year	$25 (£20) per week $103 (£80) per month $1,243 (£960) per year
• Green veggies	$1.30 (£1) per week $5 (£4) per month $62 (£48) per year	$2.59 (£2) per week $10 (£8) per month $124 (£96) per year

Chapter Two: Costs and Commitment of Keeping Mini Lops

• Pellet (1 egg cup full/ 25 kg per day for each rabbit)	$22 (£17) per year Total Food Costs Per Week: $20 (£16) Per Month: $85 (£66) Per Year: $1,016 (£785)	$44 (£34) per year Total Food Costs Per Week: $30 (£23) Per Month: $117 (£91) Per Year: $1,400 (£1,090)
• Bedding (includes newspaper, toilet paper, hay)	Free (cost of hay is given under the food column)	Free (cost of hay is given under the food column)
• Cleaning Products	25p/ week $1.30 (£1) per month $15 (£12) per year	25p/ week $1.30 (£1) per week $15 (£12) per year
• Insurance	$3.24 (£2.50) per week $13 (£10) per month $155 (£120) per year	$6 (£5) per week $25 (£20) per month $310 (£240) per year
Other Maintenance Costs: • Vet Fees (includes	$65 (£50) per year	$129 (£100) per year

Chapter Two: Costs and Commitment of Keeping Mini Lops

routine checkup and preventive vaccinations/ medical care)		
• Additional or replacement equipment (includes toys, feeders, cage, litter trays etc.)	$13 (£10) per year	$13 (£10) per year
• Boarding (for 2 week – period; cost may vary)	$6 (£5) per day for a 2 – week period $90 (£70) per year	$9 (£7) per day for a 2 – week period $126 (£98) per year
Total per week (food, bedding, cleaning materials, insurance)	$24 (£19)	$36 (£28)
Total per month (food, bedding, cleaning materials, insurance)	$98 (£76)	$145 (£112)
Total per year (food, bedding, cleaning materials, insurance, other potential maintenance expenses)	$1,356 (£1,047)	$2,000 (£1,550)

Chapter Two: Costs and Commitment of Keeping Mini Lops

Estimated Lifetime Cost (for a lifespan of 8 to 12 yrs.):

- For 1 outdoor rabbit: £11,000
- For a pair of outdoor rabbits: £16,000
- For 1 indoor rabbit: £11,000
- For a pair of indoor rabbits: £16,000

Additional Vet Expenses:

The breakdown of expenses mentioned above doesn't include vet treatment or medical procedure that could be needed if your pet mini lops suffers from an illness, injury or may need behavioral therapy.

Estimated Medical/ Vet Treatment Costs:

- **Dental Care:** £80 to 200. If your pet has some chronic dental issue then the dental cost will likely be much higher.

- **Gut Stasis Treatment:** £100 to 300 (may include X – rays or drugs). If ever your pet can't be nursed at home and requires hospitalization, it may cost around £25 per night (this will vary depending on the vet clinic).

- **Ear Problems:** Ear infections are quite common in lop breeds. Initial ear treatments may cost around £400 to 500 or more because your pet may require ongoing treatment and may involve other medical procedures such as CT scans. The cost could also reach over £1,000 if surgery is needed.

- **Limb Fracture:** £500 to 1,000 though costs could most likely exceed this range.

*Note: The figures aforementioned are taken from the estimation of costs published by the RSPCA organization in the U.K. via their website at www.rspca.org.uk.

Mini Lop Rabbit Personality

The miniature lop is behaviorally described as a docile and laid – back breed like most of its cousins and lop relatives though some people may characterize smaller breeds as more active or hyper. When it comes to the personality or behavior, keep in mind that all rabbits regardless of their size or breed family have their own set of characteristics and preferences. Needless to say, it's not good to make any generalizations because rabbits are individuals and quite unique like us humans.

Chapter Two: Costs and Commitment of Keeping Mini Lops

Whenever you're choosing a rabbit, it's best to ask the breeder, the rescuer, or from whomever you get your pet when it comes to the temperament since they are the ones who kindle and rear these cute bunnies. It's also best to take time to observe the mini lop rabbit and interact with them before choosing which one to pick.

Keep in mind that rabbits are prey animals which mean that they're generally scared of people, new environment, and new situations. It's best that you are patient with them at the onset and give your pet some time to adjust to his/ her new habitat

Chapter Two: Costs and Commitment of Keeping Mini Lops

Chapter Three: Handling, Housing, and Feeding

Living in a damp, dirty, draughty and poorly ventilated surrounding can certainly cause your mini lops to suffer and eventually become ill. Your job as an owner and responsible rabbit keeper is to not just provide them with a house that would meet their complex needs but also their behavioral needs. In addition to providing them with the right kind of living environment, you also need to make sure that they will feel 'at home' with you. How can you do this? It's not easy but it's pretty simple and it can be said in one word: commitment. Commitment and building a great relationship with your pet is part of rabbit ownership, after all, what is a hutch without a home?

Chapter Three: Handling, Housing & Feeding

When it comes to feeding, in the wild, rabbits including miniature lops are natural grazers and they primarily eat grass and other edible plants. According to vets, your pet's digestive system is built to digest grass, plants, or hay in order to properly function. A rabbit's teeth grow continuously throughout their lifetime which is why it needs to be worn down and maintained at a correct shape and length so that they can properly chew on hay, plants and treats. If they don't eat the right food their teeth will suffer serious dental problems. This chapter will provide you with feeding tips and measurements for both young and adult rabbits, how to build the right hutch for your mini lops, and also how to properly handle them so that you can enjoy quality time with your pet.

Chapter Three: Handling, Housing & Feeding

A Hutch and a Home for Your Mini Lops

A traditional small hutch or rabbit enclosure shouldn't be the permanent home of your mini lops because this wouldn't meet their needs particularly for play time, and exercise opportunities. If you just buy a standard rabbit cage for them then you will most certainly compromise their health and happiness for that matter as this can cause behavioral and health problems.

So what kind of rabbit hutch is suited for your cute and cuddly pet/s? Experts suggest that – bigger is always better! You must be able to provide a large space or living enclosure where your mini lops can freely hop around, have

Chapter Three: Handling, Housing & Feeding

playtime and exercise opportunities, have a comfortable place to rest whenever they want to, and of course, completely safe from any hazards or threats. If for some reason, you need to just confine them in an enclosure then just make sure to set a time where you can let them free around the house with your supervision.

It's also important that the living environment of your mini lops are well – ventilated and free from any potential threats such as predators (this includes your other household pets such as cats, dogs etc.), household materials, unsanitary surroundings, and extreme weather/ temperature among others.

You should also provide an additional hiding place for them so that they can have a place to go to if they feel afraid or if they simply want to have 'privacy' because if they don't they might get stressed out.

In terms of specs, your mini lops' cage should be tall and wide enough for the rabbit to stand up on their hind legs without their head touching the roof. It should also have enough space where your mini lop can lie fully stretched in any direction or at least have enough room where they can run, hop, and explore. The size of the cage will vary depending on where you're going to house them (either indoor or outdoor), the space you have available in your own home or backyard, and the mini lops' current size. In

Chapter Three: Handling, Housing & Feeding

the case of a mini lop, since they are small – sized rabbits, the cage may not need to be as large as what's being used for medium to large size rabbits, so it's up to you what size will you prefer and what size is suitable for your pet.

The main house of your pet could be attached to a so – called 'run' outside, or to an indoor pen. You can also connect it to a rabbit – proof room in your house. A rabbit – proofed room is basically a place where your rabbit can freely roam around without injuring himself and also causing problems in your house. Make sure to cover wires and cables because your mini lops will certainly chew them. Keep away potentially hazardous materials like sprays, toxic materials that your rabbit can ingest.

The purpose of attaching your pet's main shelter to an exercise run or playpen is to allow your rabbit to have a freedom to choose where he/she would spend time in at any given moment – this kind of environment can make them occupied and also satisfied.

Rabbits are generally active in the early morning and around late afternoon as well as night time. These are the times of the day where they want to play, interact with other rabbits, and also forage for their food. Make sure that the playpen or run is accessible during these times.

Chapter Three: Handling, Housing & Feeding

A Sanitary Shelter

Your rabbit's cage will most likely filled with uneaten or left over food, litter and dirt which is why it's a must that you clean their hutch every day or at least once a week especially their litter area. The whole cage/ enclosure should be thoroughly cleaned to prevent your rabbits from becoming ill. However, keep in mind that cleaning can be quite stressful for some rabbits which is why experts suggest that after you completely clean their cage, you should put back at least a small amount of used bedding in their litter area so that the smell can be familiar as it will reduce your mini lops stress due to cleaning. Always keep in mind that you should only use non – toxic cleaning materials and the cage must be dry before you put the rabbit back inside.

Companionship for Your Mini Lops

Experts suggest that every rabbit owner should take the time to handle their pets every day especially from a young age so that the rabbits will see their owners as a loving companion.

It's important that you know how to hold and pick up your rabbit – it must be gentle but firm. One of your hands should support their back and hind legs at all times, then

Chapter Three: Handling, Housing & Feeding

make sure that all their feet are held against your body and also well – supported by your other hand. If ever you're unsure on how to hold your pet mini lops, ask a vet or a breeder on how to demonstrate it for you.

If ever your rabbit needs to be kept inside their hutches for safety reasons then make sure that you still interact with them and hold them for a while every day. According to veterinarians, rabbits that aren't always being held at a young age will find human contact to be stressful and could result to fearfulness. If the rabbit becomes fearful, he/she will want to escape or become aggressive to you and other rabbit housemates. If ever your pet mini lops have some behavioral problems, ask your vet for advice. Your rabbit will most likely be referred to a behavior expert. Patience is needed in order to help your rabbit grow more comfortable around you.

Holidays and Transportations

If ever you're going away for a long vacation and you can't bring your pet rabbit with you then you have to make sure that you find someone to look after your pet's welfare. If you'll bring your pet with you and you need to board them, it's best to bring along familiar – smelling items like toys. If you have more than one then put them all in one

Chapter Three: Handling, Housing & Feeding

cage during your travel so that they can be each other's company.

Rabbit Companions

Rabbits in general are naturally interactive creatures and they usually prefer to be in the company of another similar breed or another rabbit. A rabbit that lives alone tends to develop an abnormal behavior and could be stressed out if left without any company. This is why vets and expert rabbit breeders always suggest that it's best to keep pairs of rabbits – a good combination is one male and one female (spayed/ neutered unless you want to become a rabbit breeder). Spaying or neutering them will prevent any unwanted pregnancies and it will also prevent them in fighting one another as they grow into adulthood.

If you decide to keep more than a pair of mini lops they will naturally form a sort of 'pecking order' with some animals being more dominant than the others. If the rabbits can't get away with other dominant rabbits inside their enclosure he/ she will get bullied so make sure that all of them can have a safe place to hide or they have access to other places that's still within the enclosure. When it comes to introducing rabbits, it should always be gradual. The next section will teach you how.

Chapter Three: Handling, Housing & Feeding

How to Introduce Rabbits to Each Other

Introducing rabbits is quite tricky especially for newbies like yourself. The process of 'bonding' or forming a rabbit friendship can take weeks or even months so patience is required because some are quite uncomfortable with 'bunny dates.'

Preliminary Considerations:

- **Only bond rabbits that are neutered or spayed.** This is especially if you have a male and female mini lop. You may need to wait for 2 weeks after the procedure before you can finally introduce them to one another in order to make sure that the surgery is already healed because since they are opposite sex, they'll most likely mate. Male and female bonds are usually easy to introduce compared to same – sex rabbits due to territoriality issues.

- **Do not put a new second rabbit inside the cage with your first rabbit.**
  You need to gradually introduce the new rabbit to the first one; otherwise it will cause territorial issues particularly in males. Fighting that can result to injuries is most likely to happen.

Chapter Three: Handling, Housing & Feeding

Bonding Tips:

- One of the keys to a successful bonding is 'neutral territory' – this is a space that's not familiar to either one of your rabbits. Experts suggest that the rabbits should live side by side but in separate cages. Do this method of separation for at least a couple of days or weeks before you actually put them together in a common space.

- Another tip is to bring them together for car rides. What experts recommend is to place your rabbits in separate carriers and then drive them for at least 10 minutes. After that, place them both in a litterbox filled with fresh hay so that by the end of the car ride they would most probably be huddled together in the box. This theory will make your pets realize that having a company is pleasant, and they'll be open to each other if they're not stressed. Once you've returned from the car ride, put them both in a neutral space that's not too big for both of them to ignore one another. See how they'll behave and be ready to intervene in case a fight breaks out or if there are signs of aggression.

- Increase the time of them together in a gradual way (you can start with 10 minutes then 20 minutes and so on), so that they'll be familiar with each other and make sure that they have enough food or toys to play with to avoid any fights or territorial issues. If you see them become aggressive towards one another, separate them immediately. Do not leave them alone together for the first few weeks; all meetings should be supervised until you see clear signs that they're already comfortable with one another.

- If you're already confident that they won't fight one another, you can start leaving them alone but stay within earshot to begin with because sometimes rabbits act differently when they know they're not being watched anymore. If you see them already starting to bond, you can start leaving them unsupervised for longer periods.

If your mini lops already seem comfortable being in the same neutral space, even if they're not totally interacting with one another, that's a sign that they're fine with a company. If you start seeing them groom one another then that's another sign that they've finally bonded. Grooming and snuggling are signs that bonding is successful. Once you see a solid relationship, you can start moving them into non – neutral territory.

Chapter Three: Handling, Housing & Feeding

Nutrition Guidelines for Your Pet

Your mini lops just like any other rabbits will produce 2 kinds of droppings; hard dry pellets and soft moist pellets which are also known as cecotrope. The cecotrope are soft moisted pellets that they scoop out directly from their anus. Don't mistake it for poop and don't worry because eating the so – called cecotrope right off their butts is an essential part of their diet.

Mini lop bunnies tend to take their time whenever they're eating. They usually like to forage, munch, and graze food at dawn and dusk which is why this is the best time to offer them food because they're sociable and active at these times of the day.

Chapter Three: Handling, Housing & Feeding

The amount of food your pet mini lop eats will vary individually and depends on his/ her age, health, food behavior (some likes to eat more than others), and general lifestyle. Later on in this book we will discuss about measurements for your rabbit's food that you can use as a guide.

Nutritious Food and Fresh Water

Your pet mini lops will need to be offered clean and fresh drinking water at all time. If your pet/s do not have access to fresh water or if the water is not clean, they can suffer digestive problems and can also suffer from various diseases.

Make sure to check their water supply at least two times in a day especially if you live in a cold area; if your rabbits are housed outdoors, the water could freeze up during winter, and they might not be able to drink from it. Rabbits can get dehydrated even if the weather is cold.

Good quality plants, grass or hay should be the majority of your pet's diet, and they should have access to it at all times. You will need to provide your mini lops with quality and rabbit – sized bundle of hay. The hay should be dust – free, has a sweet smell, and also fresh as much as possible. It's highly recommended that you buy a hay rack or a hanging basket because this help keeps hay or green

Chapter Three: Handling, Housing & Feeding

plants fresh and also clean. If you place a hay rack above your pet's litter tray, this might encourage them to eat more hay or other variety of plants that are edible and safe throughout the day. It's also important that you washed the leafy greens or treats that you offer to them to ensure that it's fresh and also clean.

The safest plants to offer to your pet mini lops include broccoli, kale, cabbage, parsley, carrot tops, cilantro, escarole, chard, dandelion greens, collards, spinach, lettuce, Mustard greens, endive, turnip greens, romaine, fresh herbs including basil, lemon balm, thyme, dill, fennel top, and mint among others. Never ever feed them with lawnmowed clippings because they will create problems in their digestion. Contrary to popular belief, carrots are not part of a rabbit's daily diet but if you want to offer them carrots, it should only be in small amounts. You shouldn't also feed them with root veggies, cereals, and fruits (perhaps only in small amounts and only as treats). Keep in mind that you shouldn't also offer treats that humans eat like chocolates, wafers, biscuits, candies, gummies etc. because these might upset your pet's stomach.

Commercial Pellet Diet

What you can do is to provide them with good quality rabbit pellets or commercial nuggets in order for your pet to have a varied and balanced diet. The hay/ grass

Chapter Three: Handling, Housing & Feeding

should be have the largest portion of your mini lop's diet since this is what they primarily eat. The nuggets or commercial pellets you buy should also contain high fiber levels. If you include commercial pellets in your pet's diet, you can allow around 25 grams of quality pellets per kilogram to feed for your adult – size mini lops; this measurement should be adjusted based on your pet's body weight, individual needs, age, health condition, and overall lifestyle.

If your mini lop is in its growth phase, or he/she is underweight then a larger amount of commercial pellets may be allowed. A special diet is also needed for pregnant and nursing does – consult your vet for proper measurement for these cases.

Before you add more food in their trays, it's best that your rabbit first finished what you have given them to avoid overeating as it could result to them becoming overweight. Never top up food because this will also result to them not eating enough grass/ hay which is what's more required.

Don't feed them a Muesli – style foods because it's often linked with digestion problems and it could also develop serious dental problems and obesity. Consult your vet on how you can properly and gradually change to a much healthier diet.

Chapter Three: Handling, Housing & Feeding

Work with Your Vet for Diet

It's highly recommended that you work with your vet with regards to creating a feeding plan for your pet mini lops. He/ she can help you on how you can provide the best type of diet based on your pet's current age and health condition. Your vet can also advise you on how to safely and gradually transition your pet into a much healthier diet.

Make sure to record the amount of food/ water that your pet eats and drinks every day. Monitor them for any changes in eating, drinking and drooping. For instance, if the number of poops gets less, or if your rabbit defecates very soft droopings, it's best to talk to your vet immediately as your pet could be seriously ill.

Never ever make any sudden diet changes because this will cause your pet to become ill since the food is not a familiar diet. Gradually introduce food to them and make sure to monitor how they will respond to this change so that you can adjust if need be and it will also prevent them to become overweight or underweight.

Chapter Three: Handling, Housing & Feeding

Feeding Tips and Measurements

Adult – Sized Mini Lop Diet

A balanced diet for adult sized rabbits usually consists of the following:

Grass/ Hay: unlimited or depends on your vet's recommendation.
- Timothy
- Oat
- Orchard
- Brome

Commercial Pellets: About ¼ cup per 5 pounds
Fresh Greens: at least 1 cup per 5 pounds

Benefits of Feeding Hay:
- Major source of fiber for rabbits that keep their GI tract healthy.

- Helps to develop properly aligned teeth and prevents serious dental problems

Chapter Three: Handling, Housing & Feeding

- Feeding alfalfa hay is NOT recommended because it contains high levels of calcium, calories and protein which could result to various health illnesses.

Benefits of Pellets:

- The pellet diet should contain around 18 to 20% fiber. It shouldn't contain more 16% of protein.

- Timothy – based levels is highly recommended for adult rabbits instead of alfalfa – based pellets.

- Never offer your pet mini lops with gourmet pellets because this usually contains dried fruits, corn, seeds or nuts. These ingredients are very high in starch and fat as it could create intestinal blockages and serious digestive problems.

Treats

- Avoid feeding your mini lops with commercial treats.

- You can provide baby carrots or slices of fresh fruit like apples, strawberries, pineapple or banana but only for small amounts.

Chapter Three: Handling, Housing & Feeding

- The recommended measurement for treats is only 1 to 2 tablespoons a day.

Young Mini Lop Rabbits for Diet

7 weeks to 9 months

- Unlimited Alfalfa Pellets

- Your young mini lops will need all the protein, calcium, and calories for growth

- Make sure to just feed plain alfalfa pellets. No corn, seeds, nuts or corn.
- In around 10 weeks, you can start feeding with small amounts of leafy greens such as lettuce, parsley, dandelion greens etc.

- After around four months, you can start limiting the amount of alfalfa pellets and gradually transition your young mini lops to eating hay.

- You can also provide timothy hay for neatness in your rabbit's litterbox.

Chapter Three: Handling, Housing & Feeding

9 months to 1 year

- You can gradually switch your juvenile mini lops to a more adult – sized diet.

- Start giving them limited pellets (around ¼ to ½ cup per 6 pounds). Adjust it according to their body weight.

- Gradually switch alfalfa diet to timothy pellets.

- Start feeding more amounts of green leafy veggies every day.

How to Pick – Up Rabbits

Picking up a rabbit is one of the usual things you need to do as a rabbit keeper which is why it's important that you know how to properly do this so that whenever you need to transfer your mini lop from one place to another, you can do so without making them uncomfortable or scared.

To kick things off, what you need to do is to place your palm upon them properly. Your palms should be place in your pet's abdomen; once you do that's when you lift

Chapter Three: Handling, Housing & Feeding

them up. Make sure to support the limbs or the entire body. If your pet struggle or isn't comfortable you can use your other hand to support the shoulders and/or grip its skin. Once you've successfully carried them up, you should provide support to its legs using your hand or lean it over your body.

Most newbie keepers struggle in picking up their rabbits because sometime the bunny resists. In order to avoid resistance, you need to make sure that your pet is already familiar with your scent, and you should have gradually built a relationship with your mini lop so that your pet will let you handle him/ her.

Tips when Carrying a Rabbit

This section will provide you with different methods on how you can properly carry your rabbit. Just choose and try the best way of carrying your pet so that both of you will be comfortable.

Tip #1: Hold your pet's ears and its shoulders in your right hand while placing its feet on your left arm.

Tip #2: Support your rabbit's rear with your left hand

Tip#3: Finally tuck your rabbit's head under your left elbow.

Chapter Three: Handling, Housing & Feeding

Chapter Four: Behavior and Bunny Quirks

Rabbits are highly interactive, inquisitive, and fun pets to play with but aside from their owner's company they also love to hang out and be friends with their own kind. Many rabbits enjoy gentle petting from their keepers, and they can also be trained through a positive reward based method like a clicker training. The behavior of individual rabbits regardless of their breed will vary. Their playfulness will depend on their age, individual personality and also past experiences. If ever one of your rabbits changes his/ her behavior this could mean that your pet is ill, bored, stressed

Chapter Four: Behavior and Bunny Quirks

out or lacks human/ bunny interaction. If a bunny is scared or in pain, it will definitely affect their behavior and daily habits which is why it's important that you know how to properly deal with them. This chapter will focus more on rabbit behavior and bunny quirks.

Mini Lop Bunny Behavior

If you have observed that your mini lop rabbits are doing any of the following, this means that your pet might be ill, distressed, scared, lacks human/ bunny interaction, or perhaps isn't living a 'quality pet life':

- Constantly hiding in his/ her hideout
- Altered feeding
- Chewing cage bars
- Playing with water bottle
- Over – grooming
- Hunched sitting
- Repeated circling inside the hutch
- Laziness or lethargy
- Aggressive towards people or other rabbits

If you think your pet mini lop has some changes in his/ her behavior or he/ she shows sure signs of fear, aggression or stress then better talk to your vet and do a routine

Chapter Four: Behavior and Bunny Quirks

checkup first – if your rabbit is physically cleared then your vet will most probably refer you to consult with a qualified behavior animal trainer. Never ever punish your pet if he/she behave differently, or even shout at them because they'll never understand what you're trying to teach them and your mini lops might end up more afraid or stressed out. If your mini lops are having ongoing behavioral problems make sure to talk to an expert.

Hiding Places

Always keep in mind that your bunnies must have a place to hide from things that they're scared off. They must have an area inside the enclosure where they will feel secure – this is an area that's preferably away from the sight of its outside environment, and also from the smell of predators and threats.

Experts also suggest that you should provide a platform inside the enclosure because this will allow your pet to scan their environment for any 'threats' and because this can help them feel secure. Platforms will also help your pet to be physically fit and strengthen their bones because jumping on and off a platform is a very physical weight – bearing exercise.

Chapter Four: Behavior and Bunny Quirks

If your pet mini lops have been kept in a restricted environment and has no opportunity to do such exercise, it's best to ask your vet if providing a platform will help and what size will be appropriate for your pet to prevent any injuries.

Play Time

Toys provide both physical and mental stimulation for your mini lops, and it also enables normal 'rabbit brhavior' such as chewing, chin marking, hopping, investigating, foraging and digging. Different rabbits enjoy different kinds of toys so what you can do to find out which toys your mini lops prefer you can start providing various types and see which toys your pet find interesting.

Keep in mind that you should make sure that the toys you'll provide are safe and non – toxic because your mini lops will constantly chew and play with them. In general, bunnies often love simple toys; the best thing is that these are pretty cheap and you can even improvise some toys. Here are some examples:

Chapter Four: Behavior and Bunny Quirks

- **Shredded Newspaper/ Paper bags/ Brown paper:**
  What you can do is to bundle your mini lop's fave food so that they could be curious to unwrap it.

- **Hunt or Hide boxes:**
  What you can do is to create holes in the boxes because your mini lops will surely love to squeeze on them and hide. You can also place food treats inside cardboard tubes or plastic tunnels that they can get into so that food hunting can be exciting!

Digging and Chin Marking

Digging is an innate rabbit behavior so make sure that your mini lops will have opportunities to dig up the ground. One way of doing that is by providing a 'digging box' that you can purchase from pet stores or make in your home. What you need is a plant pot or a litter box that's filled with soil, shredded paper, or child – friendly sand so that your pet will have fun.

Rabbits use their sense of smell as an important means of detection and communication which is why you should also provide objects and areas within your pet's hutch where they can scent mark using their chin secretions,

Chapter Four: Behavior and Bunny Quirks

droppings, or urine. Chin marking is another innate behavior that helps a rabbit marks his/ her territory; this will also reassure your pet that the surrounding is familiar to them. Such chin marking scents or secretions aren't detected by people or even other animals.

Keep them Safe!

Whenever you are giving new items to your pet mini lop, make sure that you have already inspected it for any potential hazards. Repair or replace any items that could be damaged already because it might injure your pet.

If you have more than one mini lop, always check if the toys you provide are enough for each of them otherwise they could become aggressive towards each other. It's also important to observe them with any new items you'll provide so that you'll know if they'll like it or not; if you think they get scare of it or is somehow threatened by it then better to remove this new item.

Make sure to regularly rotate toys so that your pets will maintain their interest in it and keep boredom at bay.

Chapter Four: Behavior and Bunny Quirks

Bunny Quirks

Here are some bunny quirks that you should know about:

Blind Spot

If you see your pet sniffing around for food that's already right in front of her, don't worry, your mini lop is not going blind because rabbits have a blind spot. Since a rabbit's eyes are positioned on the sides of their head sometimes they can't see what's right under their noses. Don't try to pat her straight into his/ her head because you may startle your pet, it's best to reach from the side or at the back of his head.

Thumping

If your pet is constantly thumping, that usually means that they're anxious about something, and they are thumping because they're trying to get your attention or they want to stay off their backs or should I say, their lops.

Chapter Four: Behavior and Bunny Quirks

"Chilled – Out Bunny"

This is when your rabbit suddenly lies down on his/her side or rolls over its back. This shows that your mini lop is in sheer relaxation.

Excitement Overload!

If your pet mini lop can't contain his/her excitement, you may notice them do a binky just like infants. They will kick up their feet and shake their body in mid – air.

Tooth – Grinding

Rabbits will grind their teeth if they're contended but if the grinding gets loud, it may denote pain.

Nipping

Rabbits may slightly bite you or nip on you if they aren't familiar with you yet but don't be offended, they're just checking if you're not a threat.

Chapter Four: Behavior and Bunny Quirks

Chin Marking

As mentioned earlier, rabbits often mark their territory or use a familiarity scent detection called chin marking. They might try to rub their chin against you or any other objects and this is normal behavior.

Poop Marking

Some rabbits will mark their territory or a certain area by pooping on them. This behavior is quite common with rabbits that haven't been surgically neutered or spayed.

Pulling of Hair

Pregnant does usually pull hair from their legs and chest to provide nesting for their kits. If your female rabbit is not neutered and she's doing this, well she's most likely pregnant.

Cecotrope Munches

Don't be shock if you see your pet reach out to her butt and come up munching – he/ she is not eating his/ her poop, but instead got a cecotropes which are fibrous pellets that's created inside the rabbit's intestine. This is an essential part of the rabbit's digestive system or their intestine also

Chapter Four: Behavior and Bunny Quirks

known as cecum. Compared to the hard fecal pellets that rabbits poop out, cecotropes are more of a gooey and soft cluster substance. However, if you find lots of cecotrope, it can be quite alarming because this could denote a health problem. Your rabbit could be obese, or the diet you are feeding your pet are too high in protein or too low in fiber

Chapter Five: Breeding Basics and Culling

Are you interested in breeding mini lops on your own? Or are you thinking about creating a consistent desirable trait among them? Well, this chapter is for you!

Breeding rabbits is a serious task that needs time, money and attention so before you become an official rabbit breeder, there are some things that you need to ponder about; are you willing to invest in learning everything you can about rabbit breeding? Do you have the space or facilities to accommodate a litter of these rabbits?

Can you handle taking care of excess or unwanted rabbits? Culling is quite difficult for newbie breeders! What

Chapter Five: Breeding Basics and Culling

kind of breeder do you want to be? I hope you consider breeding rabbits out of pure passion and not just for revenues! Regardless of your answers, there's only one thing to keep in mind, breeding should be taken seriously. This is not for fun especially for the faint hearted!

This chapter will focus on the basics of breeding so that you'll have an idea of what you're signing up for. The question is do you have what it takes to become a reputable mini lop rabbit breeder? Let us find out!

Breeding for Rabbitries

Before you make the decision of going into breeding or not, there are some things you need to know such as the pre – selection process, the mating process, the labor process and the culling process.

Pre – Selection of Parent Breed

Before you mate your rabbits, you need to ensure that the pair you selected is healthy in order to prevent passing any diseases or genetic defects to your litters or herd in the long run. Pre – selecting the parent breed is very important for any breeder looking to start a rabbitry. This will help you ensure that the future offspring possess the genetic traits so

Chapter Five: Breeding Basics and Culling

that your herd or litter will be consistent. This will also help you establish yourself as a reputable breeder. You need to be able to procreate a consistent desirable trait among your mini lop breed litters.

When it comes to the mating process, it is usually done inside the buck's male rabbit cage or hutch.

Once the doe has accepted the buck, the buck would then mount her and begin the process of mating. It usually takes about five minutes or more.

After they've mated, you can see them remove the doe and take her back to her own cage. However, if the doe refuses to mate, what you can do is to present her to another buck.

You can leave the doe inside the buck's cage for about 24 hours if possible. Bucks can already be mated at 5 months of age; however the young buck shouldn't be mated as often as an adult male rabbit.

What Expert Breeders Suggest:

- Many rabbit experts suggest mating the rabbits either early in the morning or at night time.

- You can also do a double mating wherein the doe will be mated either by the same buck with at least 10

Chapter Five: Breeding Basics and Culling

minutes interval or a different buck to ensure successful impregnation.

The Pregnancy Period

About a week or two (usually 10 to 14 days) after your pre – selected parent breeds have mated, what you can do is to see if there are embryos forming in its uterus through simply checking your doe's abdomen. Make sure to record the following:

- The date when they first mated
- How many times your rabbits have mated
- The interval period of the mating process
- Which buck/s have been mated, and to which doe/s
- When did you first check for pregnancy

You can repeat the mating cycle and present it to a buck for breeding if ever you found out that the doe didn't get pregnant after 10 to 14 days of checking its abdomen.

What Expert Breeders Suggest:

- You should not check its abdomen before the 10th day because it wouldn't be effective since the potential embryos are not quite develop yet at this stage

Chapter Five: Breeding Basics and Culling

- Avoid checking on the 15th day because this is already a delicate stage since the embryos are now starting to grow inside. This could also result to abortion or death of newborn.

Preparation for the Gestation Period

If you've found out that your doe is pregnant through palpation or perhaps an ultrasound at the vet, you can now start preparing for the labor period. You can do this around the 27th day after mating as rabbits' gestation cycle lasts for about 28 to 30 days.

Make sure to prepare a nesting box for your doe as well as the bedding materials. You also need to feed the mother doe properly at this stage to ensure that she will give birth to healthy offspring.

Since the Mini Lop is a small – sized breed, you need to provide the right measurement of feeds and clean water and this will depend on their weight/ age etc. Consult your vet to ensure if this kind of measurement is right for your breeding doe.

During the kindling period, you need to check the nest from time to time to see if your doe doesn't need any assistance (usually they don't but since you're now a

Chapter Five: Breeding Basics and Culling

breeder, you need to make sure that everything is fine). Usually does nurse their kits once a day in the morning.

What Expert Breeders Suggest:

- Check if there are any dead kits in the litter; if so then remove them immediately along with fetal sacs that the doe has not eaten because the dead kits may infect other healthy kits

- The place where you'll raise them especially at this stage should be sanitary and safe.

- When the kits eventually mature and give up milk as their main food, that's when you should start separating them from their mothers.

- Weaning occurs around twenty to thirty days after birth. This is the time when the baby rabbits begin eating pellets or solid feeds.

Chapter Five: Breeding Basics and Culling

Sorting Litters

One of the hardest aspects when it comes to raising bunnies is how to sort out or cull litters that are healthy. To cull means to choose the healthiest baby rabbits in a litter in order to control the size which also means that you will need to eventually get rid of the rabbits that won't make the cut. This is extremely difficult for new rabbit breeders because every kit is just so adorable but if you have decided to become a breeder, culling is part of the job, so to speak. It is critical that you create a strong herd right at the onset because it will be beneficial for you as a breeder in the long run. Each rabbit breeder has their own unique ways of selecting baby bunnies to keep and which to cull. Normally, those who do the "culling" are those that sell rabbits for meat and those breeders that already have more than a handful of litter in their stock.

This section will guide you on what you can do when it comes to the basics of culling and how to apply it in different stages of development.

Chapter Five: Breeding Basics and Culling

Basics of Culling Mini Lop Rabbits

Culling at Birth

The first cull usually happens when the kits are born. Mini Lops usually have varying sizes of litters, if ever the doe gave birth to more than the amount of kits you think you can handle as a breeder then you'll have no choice but to select which kits to keep and which to cull. Some experience breeders usually just keep no more than 8 kits and they usually cull the rabbits that are the smallest in size upon birth. Culling smaller kits will usually allow for more mass development within your herd. It's important to note that you don't need to cull the newborn kits right at birth if you happen to have just an average sized litter – you want them to also use each other for kindling.

Second Round of Culling

Other breeders allow some of the kits to grow at least up to 5 to 6 weeks after doing a second round of culling. Judging which one to select at this stage is much more difficult than at birth so what experts do to get the job done is to ignore the "cute parts" and focus on either culling the rabbit through the head or the bone. One way of selecting which to keep is to flip the hind foot of your Mini Lops, the hind foot should be almost as thick as they are long because

Chapter Five: Breeding Basics and Culling

you want to ensure that a thick and strong hind foot is the trait you want your future herds to carry. A fine boned rabbit is usually an undesirable trait which is why it's best to remove this rabbit through culling otherwise this certain gene or physical trait will be passed on to your future litters.

In addition to checking out the hind foot, you may also to judge the head structure. What experts usually do is to check what kind of head trait they want to have in their herd. You may want to keep rabbits that possess a thick and short skull because this will allow for the development of a bold head structure with nice curves that can be a desirable trait for your Mini Lop breeding program.

Once you've broken these body parts, you'll most probably be left with 2 to 3 offspring to grow out which is more manageable especially for starter breeders like yourself.

Final Cull

The final stage of culling usually happens before the juvenile mini lops reach adulthood (around 12 to 14 weeks old). You can easily judge which rabbits to keep or cull because their body structure is most likely developed already. You may want to keep mini lops that possess short, thick, and well – balanced body from the head to the foot. You also want to make sure that the rabbits are compact and

Chapter Five: Breeding Basics and Culling

short making the rabbit have enough balance in order for its body to properly peak from the top of the hips down to its full and well – covered hind legs. Before making judgments on which rabbit to eliminate, you may also want to feel the rabbit's body to make sure that the loin has enough width to balance the depth that the kits are carrying. Type is very important in the miniature lop breed so if ever you're unsure of yourself, never hesitate to ask the expert breeders who already have a reputation in producing quality mini lop breeds.

It's also best that you talk to as many rabbit breeders as you can especially when it comes to the selection process. Most rabbit breeders will be happy to accommodate newbies like you so follow their tips and see them in action until you get used to this practice.

Another tip is that it's best to stay away from color projects for your mini lops until you already achieved strong genetic traits among your herd or litters. If you focus on the colors, the genetic traits will be harder to establish in the long term.

Breeding is not easy at all especially when you have to literally kill these cute animals and eliminate some of them at different stages to ensure that you maintain a desirable herd for your rabbitry but as I've said earlier, it's part of breeding practices because this will ensure that the

Chapter Five: Breeding Basics and Culling

herd will be more manageable and you will keep producing constant quality pets for future mini lop keepers and also breeders. Always remember to not be discouraged if ever you made some wrong choices, and always keep in mind that there are lots of hobbyists out there with the same passion as you who will happily support and help you become a reputable mini lop breeder yourself.

Chapter Five: Breeding Basics and Culling

Chapter Six: Showing Your Mini Lop Rabbits

Since the mini lop breed is a recognized breed by various rabbit organizations and associations, you can sign up your pet for showing contents. However, your pet mini lop must adhere to the official standards of the breed in order to qualify and also win. Your pet will be judge according to its physical qualities including its weight, overall size, coat texture, colors and patterns, eyes, mask, legs, and of course it's signature lop ears. This chapter will serve as your guide if you become interested in showing your pet.

Chapter Six: Showing Your Mini Lop Rabbits

Breed Standard

The breed standard of a mini lop found in this chapter is subject to change. The Mini Lop rabbit's equivalent in the U.K. is the Dwarf Lop. There will be differences when it comes to breed standards in the U.S. and in the U.K. If you need further information on the official and updated standard of a Mini Lop, it'll be wise to check out the website of the American Rabbit Breeders Association or the British Rabbit Council.

Point System

- General Type and Condition – 30 points
- Head, Ears, Crown and Eyes – 25 points
- Coat/ Fur – 20 points
- Guard hairs – 10 points
- Color – 15 points
- Total Point – 100 points

Chapter Six: Showing Your Mini Lop Rabbits

Standard of Perfection

Size

A miniature lop is a small sized rabbit that should weigh no more than 6.5 pounds or a 3 kg. The minimum weight is around 4 pounds or a 1.93 kg.

Disqualification:

If the weight goes over the maximum weight allowed (depends on the show organization).

Body Shape

- The body must short with well – rounded loins
- Must have deep chest
- Must have relatively wide shoulders that could give a well – muscled appearance
- Short strong hind legs

Faults:

If the mini lops has a long body structure and narrow shoulders.

Chapter Six: Showing Your Mini Lop Rabbits

Ears

- Must be relatively broad
- Must be thick and well – furred
- Must be rounded at the tips
- The ears should be hanged close to the rabbit's cheeks that would appear like a horseshoe outline in the front view.
- The inside of the ears shouldn't be visible from any angle to show that it is being carried correctly.

Head

- Must be well – developed especially in male mini lops or bucks.
- The width of the head must be balance with the whole face of the rabbit.
- The space between the eyes must be balanced.
- The mini lop must have broad muzzle and full cheeks because these are desirable traits for a show.

Crown

- The basal ridge of the mini lop's ears should appear prominent when viewed from the top of its skull.

Chapter Six: Showing Your Mini Lop Rabbits

Eyes

- Round and bright eyes are desirable

Faults:

- Narrow head
- Ears are not fully lopped or properly carried back
- Ears are erect

Disqualifications:

- Runny eyes
- Wall eyes
- Malocclusion

Coat Colors and Patterns

Self – Color

White

- The body of the mini lop should be pure white.
- The eyes should be ruby red or blue in color

Chapter Six: Showing Your Mini Lop Rabbits

Black

- The body of the mini lop should be solid black in color.
- The hair shaft should be properly carried and can either have a black or blue – colored undercolor.
- The eyes must be black or dark hazel in color.

Blue

- The body of the mini lop should either have a deep or medium slate blue color
- The hair shaft should be properly carried and has a slate blue – colored undercolor.
- The eyes must be blue in color.

Brown

- The body of the mini lop should have a dark brown color
- The hair shaft should be properly carried and has a slate blue – colored undercolor.
- The eyes must be brown in color.

Chapter Six: Showing Your Mini Lop Rabbits

Agouti Pattern

Agouti

- The body of the mini lop should have a rich chestnut color with black tick pattern over its intermediate orange band.
- Must have dark slate undercolor.
- The ears must be laced in black
- The eye circles, undertail and belly must be white in color with a slate blue undercolor.

Fault: Pale top color

Chinchilla

- The undercolor must have a dark slate blue at the base.

- There intermediate portion of the pearl should have a black narrow line.

- The pearling should be clearly defined

- Top grey colors should be brightly ticked with black hairs, and the color of the fur on its neck should be relatively lighter than the rest of its body.

Chapter Six: Showing Your Mini Lop Rabbits

- The chest and flanks should be ticked with a uniform shade of pearl that's relatively lighter in color than the rest of the body.

- The eye circles should be light grey in color, and the ears must be laced in black.

Opal

- The top color should be a pale shade of blue with a fawn – colored band in between.
- The undercolor should be slate blue
- The ears must be laced in blue
- The eye circles must be white
- The underside of the tail as well as its belly should be white in color with a slate undercolor.

Shaded Pattern

Siamese Sable (Medium)

- Must have a rich sepia color to a paler shade undercolor on its face, back, ears, legs, and upper side of the tail.

Chapter Six: Showing Your Mini Lop Rabbits

- The flanks and belly should have a saddle color that shades off to a much paler color.

- The shade in the eyes and jowl should blend with its flanks and chest. The blending should be gradual.

- Must not have any streaks or blotches of sepia shadings.

- The eyes must be ruby in color.

Siamese Sable (Light)

- Has the same standard as with the medium Siamese sable, the only difference is that the color should be rich sepia.

Siamese Sable (Dark)

- Has the same standard as with the medium Siamese sable, the only difference is that the color should be very rich dark sepia.

Faults: Brown eyes and white hairs.

Chapter Six: Showing Your Mini Lop Rabbits

Siamese Sable (Dark)

- Has the same standard as with the medium Siamese sable, the only difference is that the color should be very rich dark sepia.

Siamese Smoke

- The saddle should extend from the rabbit's nape to its tail to create a smoke shade.

- The flanks, belly, and chest should have a pearl greyish beige color.

- The head, upper side of the tail, ears, and feet should match the saddle as close as possible. The shadings should be gradual to avoid streaks or blotches on the coat.

- The undercolor should match the surface shade color of the mini lop.

- The eyes must be ruby in color.

Faults: Brown eyes and white hairs.

Chapter Six: Showing Your Mini Lop Rabbits

Sealpoint

- The ears, mask, tail and feet should have a rich darkish sepia shade.

- The body should have a creamy light color.

- The eyes must be ruby in color.

Faults: Brown eyes and too much body color

Disqualification: pure grey body color

Sooty Fawn

- The body should have a fawn or orange color on its top and a whitish or bluish undercolor.

- The ears, abdomen, and tail as well as the undertail should be sooty in color or bluish black.

- The cheeks and flanks should also have sooty tips or bluish black shade.

- The eyes must be hazel in color.

Chapter Six: Showing Your Mini Lop Rabbits

Faults: If the mini lops has a very dark color; if it has light shade of tails or a color white tail (this is a serious fault).

Tan Pattern

Black Fox

- The body color must be jet – black, and the under color should also be dark.

- The feet, chest and flanks must be evenly ticked and should have guard hair that's silver – tipped.

- The eye circles should also be neatly colored and must have a pea spot in front of the ear's base.

- The line of jaw, underside of belly and tail as well as the inside of the ears should be white in color.

- The eyes should be grey or brown in color.

Blue Fox

- The body color must be medium blue, and the under color should also have the same shade.

Chapter Six: Showing Your Mini Lop Rabbits

- The feet, chest and flanks must be evenly ticked and should have guard hair that's silver – tipped.

- The eye circles should also be neatly colored and must have a pea spot in front of the ear's base.

- The line of jaw, underside of belly and tail as well as the inside of the ears should be white in color.

- The eyes can be grey, blue or brown in color.

Chocolate Fox

- The body color must be dark chocolate, and the under color should be slate.

- The feet, chest and flanks must be evenly ticked and should have guard hair that's silver – tipped.

- The eye circles should also be neatly colored and must have a pea spot in front of the ear's base.

- The line of jaw, underside of belly and tail as well as the inside of the ears should be white in color.

- The eyes can be lilac, grey, blue or brown in color.

Chapter Six: Showing Your Mini Lop Rabbits

Lilac Fox

- The body color must have a pinkish – dove color, and the under color should have a pinkish shade.

- The feet, chest and flanks must be evenly ticked and should have guard hair that's silver – tipped.

- The eye circles should also be neatly colored and must have a pea spot in front of the ear's base.

- The line of jaw, underside of belly and tail as well as the inside of the ears should be white in color.

- The eyes can be lilac in color or ruby glow.

Sable Marten Dark

- The ears, face, back and outside of the tail should have a rich dark sepia shade, and the saddle color should be well – carried on the side and must shade off to a paler color as it reaches the flanks and chest. The blending should be gradual to avoid streaks.

- There should be a soft diffusion of sepia shading.

Chapter Six: Showing Your Mini Lop Rabbits

- The rump, chest, feet and flanks should be well – ticked and must have long white hairs.

- The saddle and ears should not have any white hairs.

- The eye circles, line of jaw, belly, the underside of tail and inside of ears should be white in color.

OTHER COLOURS

Fawn

- The mini lop should possess a bright rich fawn body color.
- Must be free of blue or black guard hairs
- The chest color must match the flanks.
- The underside of jowl, undertail, inside of ears, belly and eye circles should be shaded white.

Orange

- The mini lop should possess a rich orange color that's free from any tick pattern and white colored belly.

- Must have cream undercolor

- The eyes should be hazel in color.

Steel

- The mini lop should possess a dark steel greyish color going to a slate blue undercolor.

- The tips of the fur should be steel blue or grey in color.

- The belly color should have a lighter shade to vary with the top body color.

- The ears must match with the head color, and the eyes should be hazel in color.

Butterfly

- The head markings should be white in color and must be proportionate to the body color.

- The ears must also match the body color.

- The white spots must extend from the shoulders to the tail. Patches of white may be allowed.

- The body color should be with white patches and this must extend to the chest, belly, and flanks.

Chapter Six: Showing Your Mini Lop Rabbits

Faults: Too many white hairs in the mask, and top lip

Coat Type

- The coat must be rolled back, dense, and soft with medium length of hairs

Faults:

- If the coat is too fly back or too short.
- If there's excessive white hairs in the colored areas
- White tails in sooty fawns

Disqualifications:

- Putty mask or nose
- Poor coat condition
- Bunches of white hairs or white toenails in colored areas

Chapter Six: Showing Your Mini Lop Rabbits

Chapter Seven: Health and Welfare

Rabbits often feel pain in the same way as other animals but they don't usually show any outward signs because this is natural instinct for them to not look weak as they could be preyed upon in the wild. This is the reason why lots of keepers don't have any idea that their pet is

Chapter Seven: Health and Welfare

already suffering from an illness because it's often unnoticeable especially if you don't do routine checkup. This chapter will help you detect any potential pain that your pet mini lop might experience in the future. It will also give you other health information including grooming tips to ensure that your pet is healthy inside and out!

Health Check

A sudden change of behavior in your pet mini lop could be an early indicator that he/ she is either feeling pain or is already ill. If your pet is not eating the same amount as it normally does then it's a strong sign that your mini lop is already suffering from a disease, in which case you should bring him/ her to the vet immediately.

Rabbits regardless of the breed are susceptible to various infectious and viral diseases including dental health problems. Your pet can also easily catch fatally infectious disease from wild rabbits which is why it's important that you don't let them interact with rabbits that are not domesticated pets.

Life Expectancy

Chapter Seven: Health and Welfare

A well – cared domesticated mini lops can last around 8 to 10 years or even older. The average life expectancy for rabbits is around 7 years compared to wild rabbits that can only live for about 2 years. You can help your mini lops to live a long and healthy life by simply providing them with proper diet, various exercise/ play opportunities, safety, sanitary environment, proper husbandry practices, regular vet checkup, and of course love!

Spay and Neuter Surgeries

Spaying or neutering your pet is important because of the following reasons:

- If you have an unspayed female bunny, she can have around 80% of chance of getting some kind of reproductive cancer by around 5 years of age and older.

- Rabbits that are not spayed/ neutered usually show aggression, mischief, and often become destructive due to raging hormones. It'll be hard for you to also litter train them.

- Your unspayed/ unneutered rabbits can result to unwanted litters of bunnies.

Chapter Seven: Health and Welfare

Medical Emergencies

Since rabbits are prey animals, it's natural instinct for them to hide their pain or illness which is why as their owner, it's part of your job to do a routine checkup of them so that you can be aware for any subtle signs of illness. Here are some signs to watch out for:

- Loss of Appetite
- Fewer or smaller droops
- Lethargy
- Sudden irritation or aggressiveness
- Immobility
- Diarrhea with listleness
- Bloat
- Head tilt
- Abdominal gurgling
- Loss of appetite with labored breathing
- Urine – soaked rear legs
- Lumps
- Abscesses

Grooming and Other Health Concerns

Teeth

Chapter Seven: Health and Welfare

Your pet has some dental issue if its teeth don't stop growing – this condition is known as malocclusion, and it's quite common among rabbits. Overgrown teeth should be trimmed down. Malocclusion is very painful which could cause your pet to stop eating. If you notice your pet losing its appetite and/ or he/ she is drooling then it's a sure sign that your pet has teeth or molar problems. Take your mini lop to the vet as soon as you can, and once it's resolve, make sure that you do oral checkup at least twice a year.

Ears

Whenever you groom your pet mini lop, make sure to also check his/ her ears for any wax or dirt buildup as well as any signs of redness, swelling or infection. Since mini lops ears' are hanged down, they are prone to having ear problems. Consult with your vet if you see any signs of infected ears; vets will usually examine your mini lops' ear using an instrument called otoscope since they are quite prone to ear diseases compared to rabbit breeds with erect ears.

Shedding

Rabbits shed their fur at least 4 times a year. The shedding process could take from days to weeks before completion. Some rabbits are prone to hairballs just like cats but the difference is that rabbits can't vomit the hair that they've ingested due to shedding; swallowing hairballs can cause intestinal blockage which is why you need to make sure that your mini – lop is well groomed at least every week since the miniature lop breed has a short coat.

Nails

Vets recommend that you clip your bunnies' nails at least every month or two. Make sure to rip off the end of the nails to prevent injuries. You can use a nail trimmer that's being used for cats or dogs but just make sure to not cut the quick – this is the vein running in your pet's nail and can bleed when cut.

Red Urine

The normal color of urine for healthy rabbit is usually yellow, orange and red. If you see red urine, don't panic because this can be due to the diet of your pet. As long as your bunny is spayed/ neutered, it's not an indication of blood in the urine.

Flea and Ticks

If you see any fleas or ticks in your rabbit's fur then go to your vet so that you can be prescribed with a flea/ tick

Chapter Seven: Health and Welfare

treatment. Make sure that the dosage you'll apply to your pet is safe to avoid any mishaps. Try not to use Frontline on your mini lop as it can cause fatality.

There are various steps that you can do just in case your mini lop rabbits get sick.

The first thing is to keep in close contact with a rabbit – expert vet. Whenever your pet gets sick, it's quite imperative that you have a vet who is already familiar with your rabbit's history. Just like when humans get sick, it's best to go to your family doctor or personal physician because he/ she is already familiar or has knowledge about your health status unlike if you constantly go to different doctors. This is the same with rabbits and pets in general regardless of their illness.

Make sure to familiarize yourself with your pet's normal everyday behavior because if you truly know your pet's personality, habits, etc. it's much easier for you to recognize if something's off. For instance, something could be wrong with your pet if he/ she is not eating or drinking as much, if he/ she is laying in a strange way, if he/ she is moving around uncomfortably, if he/ she is spending too much time inside the hideout, if he/ she is laying in the litter box or if he/ she is doing something that's not a common everyday behavior for your pet.

Chapter Seven: Health and Welfare

Some owners have already become very good at spotting any inconsistencies with their rabbit as the years go by. For instance, vets already know that a rabbit is suffering from stasis if he/she is laying in a weird or uncomfortable way. Some rabbits will usually press their bellies to the floor, some sit in a hunched position, some have bulging eyes while some are fidgeting and trying to shift into different positions. Keeping tabs on your mini lop's behavior will make it easier to detect and prevent any health problems before it gets worse.

GI Stasis: A Very Common Illness of Rabbits

When it comes to this common illness, keep in mind that it doesn't only affect your rabbit's digestion but also its GI motility. If the ileus has been gradually coming on for quite some time, you'll see fewer and smaller feces, which is why you should know what kind of poop your rabbit produces so that you can detect the inconsistency. If it's a poop scoop size then that's usually an indicator of digestive or intestinal problems. You should make sure to check your pet's litterboxes and take note of the size, characteristics, and amount of their normal feces so that you will be aware if there's a possible problem.

Another early sign of digestive problem is when your pet doesn't finish eating the normal amount of food you give

Chapter Seven: Health and Welfare

him/ her, or if ever your pet completely lost its appetite. Knowing your pet's normal eating and drinking habit is essential so that you can take action immediately as soon as you notice a change in their eating or pooping habits.

What To Do?

If you think your pet mini lop has some gastro – intestinal problems, one of the first things to do is to determine if your pet's tummy is creating any sound. The normal digestive tract of a healthy rabbit should make a little noise that you can hear. It usually sounds like gurgling or water swishing. Make sure to also familiarize yourself with the sound of your pet's digestive tract so you can easily recognize if there's any problem.

There could be a problem if you don't hear any sound at all. On the other hand, if you hear lots of gut sounds, these could be signs that the ileus is causing gas. In some cases, the gurgling of a bunny's stomach can be heard across the room!

Do take note that not all cases of ileus involve gas but many do, and usually the treatment for this condition is the same whether there's gas or not. If you're quite certain that there could be digestive problems then treatment must be taken immediately.

Chapter Seven: Health and Welfare

The medication that you need to administer is called Simethicone – this is a drug that can also be used for both children and adults. The common brand names are Gas X and Phazyme, and you can buy it over – the – counter.

You don't need to worry about doing something that could make your rabbit's condition worse because Simethicone is usually a good first aid drug that doesn't cause any harm as long as you'll give the right dosage for your pet. This drug is usually very effective and must be included in your pet's first aid kit. You'll need to mix the drug with water as this will help hydrate your rabbit's stomach and intestines.

Below are some tips when it comes to doing self – medication for your pet if you think he/ she is suffering from GI stasis. It's important to take note that the tips below should not take the place of taking your mini lop to the vet, this can come in handy for first aid purposes only. You should still have your pet check by the vet even if this medication made your rabbit feel better.

Listen for gut sounds: If there's no sound, then it could mean that your pet has ileus problems. On the other, if there's loud gut sounds, it could mean that there's lots of gas inside their stomach.

Chapter Seven: Health and Welfare

Mix the medicine. You need to first mix a 125 mg of Simethicone tablet with around 2 ½ cubic centimeter of water. After you do that you can transfer into a syringe, and place it in the corner of your pet's mouth before carefully squeezing the plunger. If ever your rabbit resists, you may need to wrap your rabbit in a towel so that he/she has no choice to resist.

Massage your pet's stomach. Once your rabbit has already taken in the medicine, you can start gently massaging its stomach for at least a few minutes.

Keep your rabbit warm. If your rabbit feels cool to the touch, what you can do to help warm it down or regulate its temperature is to provide a heat pad and set it on a low level. Put a towel on top of the heat pad so that your pet won't be heated too much. As the ileus continues, your rabbit may become cold which is why you need to help warm them down for at least 10 to 15 minutes. This usually often helps their digestion because the blood can be redirected to the gut than having to help regulate the rabbit's body temperature.

Chapter Seven: Health and Welfare

Repeat administering the medicine (if necessary). If your pet is still not feeling well after 45 minutes, you may repeat giving oral hydration of Simethicone again. Do it at least twice or thrice every 45 minutes if in case the rabbit is still not feeling well. If symptoms persist, you should take your pet to the vet as soon as possible. You can also try offering your pet with hay or green veggies. You can also encourage your pet to gently move as this can help get the gastro – intestinal tract moving.

Usually, if you've already detected the problem early, you can self – medicate your pet and get their GI tract moving again after administering oral hydration.

Chapter Seven: Health and Welfare

Glossary of Rabbit Terms

Agouti – A type of coloring in which the hair shaft has three or more bands of color with a definite break between.

Albino – A pink-eyed, white-furred rabbit.

ARBA – The American Rabbit Breeders Association; an organization which promotes rabbits in the United States.

Awn – The strong, straight guard hairs protruding above the undercoat in angora breeds.

Bangs – Longer fur appearing at the front base of the ears and on top of the head in some woolen breeds.

Base Color – The color of the fur next to the skin.

Bell Ears – Ears that have large tips with distinct fall.

Belt – The line where the colored portion of the coat meets the white portion, just behind the shoulders.

Blaze – A white marking found on the head of the Dutch rabbit; the shape is wedge-like.

Bonding – A term used to describe two rabbits that have paired up together.

BRC – The British Rabbit Council, formed from the British Rabbit Society and the National Rabbit Council of Great Britain in 1934.

Broken Coat – Guard hairs that are missing or broken in places, exposing the undercoat.

Buck – An intact male rabbit.

Buff – A rich, golden-orange color.

Caecotroph – Pellets of semi-digested food eaten from the anus for nutrition reasons.

Chinning – Rubbing the chin on objects of people to spread scent from glands under the chin.

Cobby – A term meaning stout or stocky in body; short legs.

Condition – The overall physical state of a rabbit in terms of its fur, health, cleanliness, and grooming.

Crossbreeding – Mating two different breeds.

Cull – The process of selecting the best rabbits from a litter and selling or slaughtering the rest.

Dam – A female rabbit that has produced offspring.

Doe – An unaltered female rabbit.

Flat Coat – Fur lying too close to the body, lacking spring and body as noted by touch.

Fryer – A young meat rabbit no more than 10 weeks of age and weighing less than 5 pounds.

Gestation – The period of time between breeding and birthing (or kindling).

Guard Hair – The long, coarser hairs in a rabbit's coat which protect the undercoat.

Herd – A group of rabbits.

Inbreeding – Breeding of closely related stock.

Junior – A class of rabbits referring to those under 6 months of age.

Kindling – The process of giving birth to baby rabbits (kits).

Kindling Box – A box provided for a pregnant rabbit so she can make a nest and give birth.

Kit – A baby rabbit.

Line Breeding – A breeding program in which rabbits that are descended from the same animal are bred.

Litter – A group of young rabbits born to one doe at the same time.

Loose Coat – Fur conditions in the undercoat, often coupled with smooth hair resulting in not so good texture.

Malocclusion – A misalignment of the rabbit's teeth.

Molt – The process of shedding or changing the fur, happens twice each year.

Nest Box – A box provided for a pregnant rabbit so she can make a nest and give birth.

Nursing – The process of kits suckling milk from the dam's teats; usually occurs twice a day.

Peanut – A rabbit with two dwarf genes; usually fatal.

Pelage – The fur coat or covering in a rabbit.

Pellets – May refer either to the rabbit's poop or its food.

Quick – The pink part of the nails/claws that contains the blood vessels and nerves.

Racy – Referring to a slim, slender body and legs.

Saddle – The rounded portion of the back between the rabbit's shoulder and loin.

Self-Colored – A fur pattern where the hair colors are the same all over the body.

Sire – A male rabbit that has produced offspring.

Thumping – The practice of banging or stomping the hind legs on the ground to make a loud, thudding noise.

Ticking - A wavy distribution of longer guard hairs throughout the rabbit's coat.

Weaning – The process in which baby rabbits become independent of their dam, transitioning to solid food

Index

A

Abscesses	73
accessories	27
active	22
age	8, 67, 118
alfalfa	48
altered	8
American Rabbit Breeders Association	116
animal movement license	18
antibiotics	72, 74
antiseptic	49
ARBA	19, 66, 116

B

baby	22, 79, 118, 120
back	119
bacteria	28, 49, 71
bedding	30, 75, 77
belly	118
birth	118, 119
birthing	118
bladder	72
blood	49, 75, 76, 119
body	49, 78, 79, 117, 119
bowls	28
box	22, 72, 118, 119
BRC	19, 66, 117
breathing	75
breed	18, 67
breed standard	61
breeding	118
breeds	61, 116, 117
British Rabbit Council	117
broken	117

brush 68

C

cage 7, 22, 28, 72, 73, 78
care 23, 70
causes 72, 75, 79
chin 117
cleaning 68
coat 9, 48, 77, 116, 118, 119, 120
coloring 116
condition 75, 77
conjunctivitis 71
convulsions 75, 79

D

dangerous 8, 72
defecate 47
diet 23
discharge 71
disinfect 79
disorientation 72
docile 8, 23
doe 118
dogs 8

E

E. Cuniculi 79
ears 71, 76, 116
exercise 28
export 18

F

feeding 37

female	8, 117
fever	48, 74, 75, 76
fiber	18, 29
fluid	74
food	68, 73, 75, 117, 119, 120
fur	72, 116, 117, 119, 120

G

genes	119
grooming	68, 78, 117
guard hairs	116, 120

H

habitat	26, 27, 77
hair	72, 78, 116, 119
hay	29, 48, 77
head	71, 78, 79, 116
head tilt	72, 79
health	21
healthy	22

I

illness	77
import	18
infection	49, 71, 74, 76, 77, 78
infectious	71, 75
inflammation	72, 73, 74, 75
intact	117

J

judging	68

K

kindling 118
kits 118, 119

L

legs 78, 117, 119
lesions 78, 79
lethargic 22
lethargy 74, 75, 76
license 17, 18
litter 21, 30, 48, 72, 117
loin 119

M

male 8, 117, 119
malnutrition 78
marking 116
materials 28
meadow hay 29
meat 18, 118
medications 74, 79
milk 119
mites 77
mosquitos 76
Myxomatosis 76

N

nails 49, 119
neck 77
nervous 8
nest 118, 119
noise 119
nutrition 117

O

offspring	117, 119
organization	116

P

pair	8
parasites	76
Pasteurella	71
pattern	119
permit	17, 18
pets	9, 10, 17, 18
play	22
pneumonia	48, 74
Pneumonia	74
pregnant	118, 119
prize	68
probiotics	72
pus	72, 74

Q

quarantine	72
quick	49

R

rabies	18
regulations	17, 18, 67
reproductive	72
requirements	27
respiratory	71

S

sanitation	72, 73, 76, 78

scent 117
schedule 67
self 68
selling 18, 117
shedding 119
shoulders 116
show 61, 75
showing 61
size 7
skin 73, 77, 116
sneezing 71
social 7
solid 120
spayed 17
standard 61
stress 77, 78
styptic powder 49
symptoms 75, 79

T

teeth 119
temperature 49
texture 118
ticks 76
time 22, 24, 29, 68, 69, 118
timothy hay 29
treatment 72, 73, 74, 76, 78, 79
type 29, 30, 38, 48, 74, 116

U

unaltered 117
undercoat 116, 117, 118
urinate 47
urine burn 30, 73

V

vegetables 37
viral 74, 75, 76

W

water 68, 75
weight 74, 75
wound 74

Photo Credits

Page 1 Photo by user Myxi via Flickr.com,

https://www.flickr.com/photos/myxi/413023943/

Page 4 Photo by user Mark Philpott via Flickr.com,

https://www.flickr.com/photos/fftang/9634858561/

Page 15 Photo by user Mark Philpott via Flickr.com,

https://www.flickr.com/photos/fftang/14149623461/

Page 27 Photo by user Myxi via Flickr.com,

https://www.flickr.com/photos/myxi/412998650/in/photostream/

Page 29 Photo by user Franie Frou Frou via Flickr.com,

https://www.flickr.com/photos/franie/3133433172/

Page 38 Photo by user Mark Philpott via Flickr.com,

https://www.flickr.com/photos/fftang/6701344929/

Page 49 Photo by user Franie Frou Frou via Flickr.com,

https://www.flickr.com/photos/franie/279802508/

Page 60 Photo by user Nikki Gibson via Flickr.com,

https://www.flickr.com/photos/dancer4life17/5184324108/

Page 71 Photo by user Franie Frou Frou via Flickr.com, https://www.flickr.com/photos/franie/523631630/

Page 89 Photo by user Thomas Armour via Flickr.com, https://www.flickr.com/photos/thomasarmour/5499404423/

References

"Mini Lop Rabbits" – Rabbit Breeders

http://rabbitbreeders.us/mini-lop-rabbits

"Dwarf Lop And Mini Lop Rabbit" – BurkesBackyard.com.au

https://www.burkesbackyard.com.au/fact-sheets/pets/pets-pet-care-native-animals/dwarf-lop-and-mini-lop-rabbit/

"The Mini Lop Rabbit" – RabbitMatters.com

http://www.rabbitmatters.com/mini-lop.html

"Everything You Need To Know #1: Mini Lops" – PrettyPetsWorld.com

https://prettypetsworld.weebly.com/blog/everything-you-need-to-know-1-mini-lops

"Mini Lop Rabbit Breed" – Lafeber.com

https://lafeber.com/mammals/mini-lop-rabbit-breed/

"Keeping a Mini Lop" – MiniLops.info

http://www.minilops.info/keeping-a-mini-lop

"Mini Lop Diet" – MiniLops.info

http://www.minilops.info/mini-lop-diet

"How to Raise a Lop Eared Rabbit" – PetPonder.com

https://petponder.com/how-to-raise-lop-eared-rabbit

"Rabbit Care & Behavior Information" – ColumbusRabbit.org

http://columbusrabbit.org/chrsbooklet.pdf

"Sorting Mini Lop Litters" – MSRBA.net

http://www.msrba.net/Archive/Newsletters/Mini%20Lop%20Article.pdf

"Costs and Time Involved in Keeping Rabbits" – RSPCA.org.uk

https://www.rspca.org.uk/adviceandwelfare/pets/rabbits

"Mini Lop" – Wikipedia.org

https://en.wikipedia.org/wiki/Mini_Lop

www.ingramcontent.com/pod-product-compliance
Lightning Source LLC
Chambersburg PA
CBHW060840050426
42453CB00008B/762